life lessons
by Agnes

Written and illustrated by
Claire Culliford

For Mum,

who taught me the beauty of words and

never to give up on my dreams.

Agnes and I love you so much.

X

The world we live in can make it hard at times

to remember what is really important in life.

This book is designed to share Agnes' love,

which knows no bounds, with everyone who

reads it. My hope is that it will also serve as a

reminder of the simple things that make your

heart sing, on those days when life gets in the

way of... well, life!

Agnes is my little dog,

But she's not just any pet.

Agnes is the very best friend

I could ever get.

Agnes has her very own personality.

In her special way, she teaches me about

How life should be.

Agnes has taught me to ...

Get plenty of exercise,

Enjoy every mouthful of food,

Be thankful for the simple things,

Like long walks in the woods.

Make time for playing every day,

Give lots of big hugs,

Constantly try new things,

Curl up and sleep on rugs.

Take a keen interest in whatever's around,

Everything and everyone,

Because curiosity leads to learning,

As well as lots of fun.

Lick away sad, salty tears,

Protect those I love most,

Chill out as much as possible,

Go crazy at the sound of post!

Keep precious things in a safe place,

Sniff out wonderful treats,

Shake my behind when I'm ecstatic,

And skip along on my feet.

Agnes and I have never talked,

In any human words.

We communicate in other ways,

Like high fives and chasing birds.

From barking loud to cuddling up,

Hide and seek around a chair,

The language of love is the very best kind

And it's the one we share.

Agnes is my little dog,

But she's not just any pet.

Agnes is the very best friend

I will ever get.

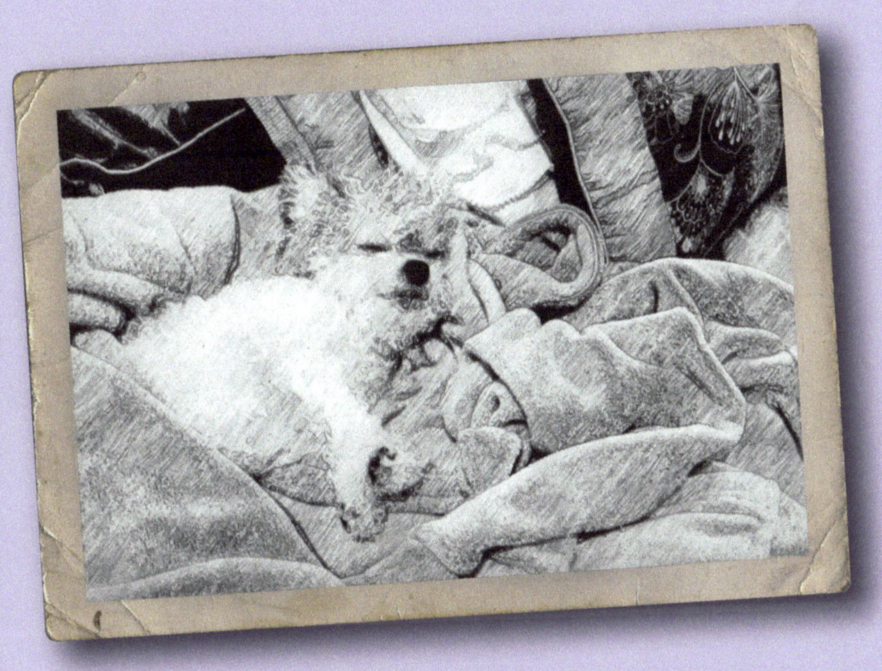

She's by my side day and night,

Through rain, hail, and sunshine,

Helping me make memories

To last a whole lifetime.